PHANTOM POETRY

A collection of poems inspired by the tale of The Phantom of the Opera

KAYLA LOWE

Phantom Poetry. © 2018 by Kayla Lowe. All Rights Reserved.

All rights reserved. No part of this book may be reproduced in any form or by any electronic or mechanical means including information storage and retrieval systems, without permission in writing from the author. The only exception is by a reviewer, who may quote short excerpts in a review.

Cover designed by Kayla Lowe

This book is a work of fiction. Names, characters, places, and incidents either are products of the author's imagination or are used fictitiously. Any resemblance to actual persons, living or dead, events, or locales is entirely coincidental.

Kayla Lowe
Visit my website at www.kaylalowe.com

Printed in the United States of America

First Printing: Jan 2018
Kayla Lowe

❦ Created with Vellum

Much thanks to all the Phans and readers who encouraged me to create this Phantom poetry collection. This is for you.

PREFACE

For those of you who aren't acquainted with the tale of *The Phantom of the Opera*, a bit of background summary is probably conducive to better understanding the poetry contained within this volume. While you may (and are indeed encouraged) to derive your own special meanings from the poems, if you'd like to follow along better, it helps to familiarize yourself with the storyline of *The Phantom of the Opera*.

First of all, there've been many adaptations of this beloved tale over the last century, but the inspiration for these poems was primarily gleaned from the original novel by Gaston Leroux and the musical and stage versions created by Sir Andrew Lloyd Webber. However, many of the poems could also easily apply to the Yeston/Kopit or Rosen and Schierhorn stage adaptations as well as a number of film adaptations, so whoever your Phantom face claim, feel free to imagine as you wish. (If you're unfamiliar with all the different versions of Phantom out there and would like to learn more, feel free to contact me via one of the channels listed in the *About the Author* section of this book, and I'd be happy to point you in the direction of some excellent resources. There's nothing I love more than discussing Phantom and introducing newbies to the Phandom. There's simply too much for me to record here. I daresay if I tried to list all the Phantom adaptations in circulation, that information alone would take up a book longer than this collection of poetry.)

Back to the matter at hand, though...

While I would never attempt to condense Leroux's book into a single paragraph, I will offer you a few basic facts that should give you an elementary understanding of the storyline. (For the best reading experience, I truly do encourage you to read Gaston Leroux's original novel and then maybe watch a few film and stage adaptations, but I digress..)

Christine Daae was the daughter of a Swedish violinist. She was said to have the voice of an angel, and her papa was known throughout the land for his exceptional skills on the violin. They sang in traveling fairs until Papa Daae got sick and died, leaving his young daughter an orphan. During the time that her papa was alive, however, he and Christine vacationed by the sea in the summer, and it was there that she met her childhood sweetheart, the Vicomte Raoul de Chagny. The most memorable scene between Christine and Raoul was when the young vicomte rushed into the ocean to rescue her red scarf that the wind had ripped from her hands.

After Christine's father died, she was sent to sing at the Palais Garnier as a member of the chorus. It was there that the lonely orphan encountered the "Angel of Music." Her papa often told her and young Raoul stories of an angel of music, and upon his deathbed, he promised Christine that he would send the Angel of Music to her. Christine carried this promise in her heart, and when an unseen voice began to speak to her from beyond the walls of her dressing room, she naturally assumed that it was the voice of the Angel of Music

PREFACE

when, in fact, it was the voice of Erik, otherwise known as the infamous Phantom of the Opera.

Erik was a disfigured man who sought refuge from the cruelty and taunting of mankind in the bowels of the Opera House. He'd helped build the Opera House and had constructed himself a secret home beyond the famous underground lake that lies beneath it. A musical genius who composed his own operas, Erik couldn't resist reaching out to the young girl when he heard her clear soprano voice. He pretended to be her Angel of Music and provided her with voice instruction until her instrument was toned to perfection. He promised to make her the prima donna of the Opera House, but he was a strict teacher and held his protegee to an uncompromising set of rules. Erik, dubbed the Phantom for the mishaps he caused around the Opera House (most notably the extortion of a salary he exerted from the managers), lived vicariously through Christine and her success, but he didn't count on falling in love with the young ingenue.

He began to hope that Christine might one day return his love and come to see him as a man, but then the Vicomte came back into the picture after many years of separation. Christine seemed to be just as enamored with Raoul as she had been back in their childhood days, which prompted the Phantom to take action by luring her to his home underground where she unmasked him and set in motion all the tragic events that followed. The entirety of said events and their outcomes vary slightly depending upon which version you watch or read. However, for purposes of this collection, we will err towards Leroux and Webber's interpretations.

These poems, organized in three chapbooks, detail the emotions of the characters during each time frame. *Thoughts of Summertime* captures Christine and Raoul's budding love, *Soul Singing* encapsulates the fantastical relationship between

PREFACE

Christine and her Angel of Music, and *In the Bleak Midwinter* showcases the drama and turmoil each character experiences as a result of this tragic love triangle.

Now, without further ado, I encourage you to turn the page and begin this poetic journey...

THOUGHTS OF SUMMERTIME

CHRISTINE

CHRISTINE

SWEET ABANDON

the wind kissed her cheeks
    soft as petals
    freshly fallen
    cherubic
    rosy

she raised her hands to touch the sky
    twirling, face upturned
    in sweet abandon
    the long golden ringlets
    that were her halo
    swaying down her back

free...
    lost...
    for one moment in time

              . . .

—sweet abandon

ON PAPA'S KNEE

on papa's knee
    was the only place
    she wanted to be
    tinkling laughter
    girlish giggles

bursting forth
    with the true joy
    only a child can know

she hummed along
    to the strains of the violin
    he played
    watching as his arms
    moved back and forth
    to coax the notes forth
    with the bow
    a twinkle in his eye

. . .

her voice opened in song
    gypsy melodies
    and hymns pouring forth
    in such innocence
    and pureness of sound and soul

—on papa's knee

WANDERERS

will we be going
    to the fair?
    Oh, please say yes!
    you promised
    to take me there

i'll dance and sing
    whilst you accompany
    me with your own singular flair

the crowds will love us
    and pay alms to our music
    just there
    in your upturned cap
    then we'll dine and sup
    as we're wont to do
    before walking along the beach

    hand in hand
    father and daughter

content in our wandering life

—wanderers

ANGEL OF MUSIC

i sit by your feet
    like an obedient puppy
    eager to hear more
    dark stories of the north
    as you play the violin
    strumming it gently
    in the background to accompany
    your words until they and the music
    combine to become one

you speak of a heavenly being
    who visits every great musician
    the angel of music

how i long to see him
    i imagine him glowing
    in heaven's light

. . .

my tiny voice
    will it ever be enough
    to warrant a visit
    from one so pure?

you assure me that it is
    so i dream and long for that day

—angel of music

SIMPLE ELEGANCE

she found joy in simple things
    burlap and bows
    ribbons and lace
    dust fairies dancing in the sun's rays

she realized there
    was an elegance
    and refinement
    in the understated
    grace was she

—simple elegance

THINK OF ME

please promise me
    my love
    that you'll think of me fondly

for as I lie in the grass
    daydreaming, the sun kissing my skin
    my cheeks blush
    with thoughts of you

—think of me

DAYDREAM WALTZ

a breeze blows through
    the open window and
    softly rustles
    the netting around my bed

i watch the thin fabric
    sway as if it's
    dancing

as i dream of dancing
    a waltz
    with you
    my prince

—daydream waltz

GHOSTS OF THE PAST

damask curtains
    a tinkling music box
    the tufted cushions
    of a wingback chair
    all relics of
    a bygone era

i wonder what scenes
    have played out
    in this very space
    what secrets it holds

—ghosts of the past

RED SCARF

a frayed red scarf
    irrelevant
    a tattered old rag to the rest of the world

to her though
    it was worth its weight in gold
    gifted from a father
    rescued by a childhood sweetheart

she ran her fingers
    along its ragged edges
    and smiled
    a wistful smile
    filled with nostalgia
    and memories of
    paternal violin strings

          . . .

—red scarf

PRIMA DONNA

soaring to the heights
    of heaven
    glittering diamonds
    extravagant tiaras and headpieces
    lavish costumes
    poster features
    the adoration of the masses
    the prima donna

how her heart yearned
    to one day reign as such!
    worthy of the angel of music

—prima donna

CHILDHOOD FRIEND

heart tripping
    speeding up
    in beats that fill my ears
    my mouth curves upwards
    smiling

squinting
    could it be?

is it really you
    my childhood friend?

his eyes sparkle
    the same twinkle they held
    in childhood days

              . . .

KAYLA LOWE

i glimpse the boy
    he once was
    hidden beneath
    his mature visage
    and my heart melts
    with fondness

—childhood friend

RECONNECTION

blushes
    shy glances

our interaction
    is different from before
    pinpoint it not
    the change
    'tis there nonetheless

running hand in hand
    pretending
    play-acting
    all has given way
    to flutterings
    and a pleasant awkwardness

                  . . .

KAYLA LOWE

that promises of things to come

—reconnection

DREAMS OF SUMMER

art thou dreaming
   the same dream
   that mine heart dreams?

gurgling brooks and streams
   walks down the lane

by a simple summer cottage
   by the sea

hand in hand
   whiling away the hours
   in sunlight and daydreams
   as we once did

—dreams of summer

ALL I ASK

the soft feeling
    of the contours of
    our hands
    entwined together

stroking my cheek
    causing a blush to stain them
    as i glance downwards
    content in your affection

simple gestures
    nothing grand is needed
    such is
    all i ask of you

—all i ask

BLOOMING IN LOVE

daises and wildflowers
    orchids and peonies
    light and fragrant
    like our love

pretty
    striking to look at
    not yet wilted
    by the cares of the world

wilt thou protect
    my blossoms
    and make sure
    that i always bloom?

give me water

and i will flourish
under your love

—blooming in love

RAOUL

AURA

she was like
    the summer breeze
    a gentle respite
    from the norm

not exactly wild
    yet untamed
    her aura glowing
    in soft hues

twirling among
    countless others
    she stands out
    every time

brighter

glowing
with a special light

—aura

ANGEL BELLS AND GIGGLES

playful lilies
    amidst a spray of curls
    yellow—nay, golden

they catch in my fingers
    as i touch them with reverence

she giggles
    a tinkling sound
    of thousands of angel bells
    lightly struck from the heavens

how could anyone
    not revere one
    so perfect in her
    childish innocence?

. . .

—angel bells and giggles

SUMMERS AGO

i met my love long ago
    lily pad kisses
    sparkle and shine

she danced in the rain
    and from that moment
    i knew i wanted her
    to be mine

my heart crashed
    within mine chest
    like the lofty waves
    crashing upon the shore
    where the wind
    stole her scarf
    and i drenched myself
    to retrieve it

        . . .

in my madness
    in the first throes of love

i'd do anything for her
    my love and childhood sweetheart
    from all those summers ago

—summers ago

VIOLIN LESSONS

back and forth
    to and fro
    dragging the bow
    over the tautly strung strings

i would practice
    all day if it delighted
    you and caused your
    eyes to glow like so

the instructor nods
    your father
    you smile your impish smile
    before grabbing my hand
    and pulling me off and into the sand
    where we frolic
    in carefree leisure

        . . .

those dusky hours
    of the evening
    going on twilight
    after the violin lessons

—violin lessons

FIRST LOVE

there's something special
    about that first love
    i've searched the world over
    and never found another like you

none could compare
    to the one who affected
    those first stirrings of
    passion within my young breast

maybe it was the sand
    or the sun
    or the sea
    but for whatever reason
    you have always stayed with me

—first love

STRAIGHT TO THE HEART

my heart stopped beating
    time stood still
    blinking
    do my eyes deceive me?

or is that you upon the stage?
    in all your glorious splendour
    gone are your gawky limbs

curves
    alabaster white skin
    creamy and smooth as milk
    a vision to behold
    in white silk, lace and taffeta
    diamonds glittering in your hair

                  . . .

KAYLA LOWE

a voice pure enough
    to cut through the air
    like an arrow
    pointing straight to my heart

—straight to the heart

NOBILITY NAUGHT

born of nobility
    i might be
    yet not one bit of
    my pedigree
    matters to me

when i'm in the warm
    glow of your presence
    fragrant blossoms
    wilt under your light
    even they know they
    can't hold a candle
    to you, my love

safety
    security
    castles
    in the air

    or the sand

all will be yours
    if you agree
    to take my hand

—nobility naught

MY BROUGHAM'S WAITING

my brougham's waiting
    come away with me
    we'll go wherever
    your heart leads us

don't shy from me darling
    wilst thou come?

thick lashes downcast
    in modesty only endear you
    to mine heart further
    and cause it to beat incessantly
    and take wing in flight

my brougham's waiting

                . . .

KAYLA LOWE

—my brougham's waiting

NOTHING COMPARES

patron of the arts
    grandiose architecture
    golden statues
    in lavish ornamentation

aged wines and cheeses
    family heirlooms
    shoes polished to a sheen
    all these delicate luxuries

none of it compares
    to the beauty that is you
    or to the fond memories
    we share with just one look

—nothing compares

OUR TREASURE

this band
    is more than a
    striking piece
    of workmanship
    or extravagant jewelry

it's a band of hope
    that my heart holds
    to enfold yours
    within my own

my heart is big enough
    to safely encircle yours
    and keep it safe within
    my own chest

i'll give you the key

> so that only you
> hold the power
> to unlock it

our dearest treasure

—our treasure

PROTECT YOU

a great abyss
    a gaping chasm
    separating my love and i

stations apart
    worlds apart
    yet none of that matters
    when i look into
    the crystalline depths of your eyes
    that smile at me
    with gentleness
    and so much sweetness
    that my heart hurts
    to behold it

i want to shelter it
    and protect it always

. . .

—protect you

BEYOND MORTAL

sunshine and rainbows
    magical things
    that can't be touched
    by a mere mortal
    that's what thou art

thy walk alone
    is a song
    and thy presence
    the most lingering of melodies

a princess from
    the fairy tales of old
    and i long to be your
    knight in shining armor

upon my gallant steed

    i'll place thee
    to whisk thee away
    to my palace
    and drip thee in gold

—beyond mortal

WILLFULLY BLIND

i am willfully blind
    when i'm with you
    content to see nothing
    but the light that you emit

willfully blinded
    by the rest of the world
    and all its cares and troubles

for within your eyes
    i see the ocean
    where we once played
    and laid upon the sand

in childhood freedom
    if i could keep you always

i'd stay blind forever

—willfully blind

WHERE ARE YOU?

where have you gone
    my wandering love of mine?

i've checked behind stage doors
    props and scenes
    now to your dressing room
    i go in hopes of securing your hand

i'll not rest
    no, i'll be much aggrieved
    that's the state
    your love has me in

but you are nowhere to be found
    my heart ails me
    and i'll not be content

until i find
just where my love went

—where are you?

FIREWORKS

bursts of color
    decorating the sky

they reflect in our eyes
    i grasp your hand

we smile
    our eyes locking
    no need
    for such propaganda

we are
    the fireworks

—fireworks

SOUL SINGING

CHRISTINE

MAGIC IN YOUR VOICE

there's a magic in your
    voice

that speaks to my soul;
    it lifts me higher
    and encourages me to
    fly
    soaring higher than
    i ever aspired to go

it understands feelings
    i can't put into words,
    luring me to believe
    you truly are
    my other half

    —magic in your voice

THE VIOLIN AND BOW

we are so in tune
    it's as if we fell from
    the same star
    were plucked from
    the same garden
    and are embers of
    the same flame

we burn as one and
    complete one another

i am
    the violin
    and you
    the bow
    that plays me
    causing me to sing sweet melodies

of our souls as one

—the violin and bow

CALLING THE ANGEL

angel of music
    come to me!
    grant me your glory
    your gift
    of song

i want to behold
    all the wonder that is you
    your halo
    your streaming hair of white
    your body draped with the finest silk

are your eyes golden?
    do they reflect the dawning sun
    and all of heaven's promises?

your voice is smoother

    than the most finely crafted
    violin
    it hypnotizes me
    with its unearthly beauty
    that can't be of this world

how awed i would be
    to be in your presence
    and to feel your light
    shining on me

—calling the angel

SOULMATES

our souls met
    long before our eyes ever did
    we connected
    on a spiritual level
    and forged
    a special bond
    of knowing each other's true selves

it wasn't about beauty or the lack thereof
    rather, our love was born
    of the deepest and purest kind
    through getting to know each other's
    hearts and minds

such a true connection
    can never be severed
    we are soulmates

now and forever
in every life our souls will find each other

—soulmates

FROM WHENCE DO YOU COME?

you come to me in my dreams
    whispering words of love and promise
    the cadence of your voice
    hypnotizing me

your ethereal being only seeks me at night;
    though my sleeping self thrills at your touch
    my waking form fears those
    remembered moments

the day passes by in a mere façade
    a hazy blur
    during which i both dread and long for the night
    when i know you will come for me again

but are you an angel sent from heaven

or hell?

—from whence do you come?

DANGEROUS VOICE

your voice
    calls to me
    like a sweet siren song
    pulling me up
    into unforeseen danger

i go willingly
    following wherever
    it may lead
    deceived
    enraptured
    by the
    Angel in Hell
    but at this point
    i care not
    i would follow that voice
    to the ends of the earth

                . . .

KAYLA LOWE

—dangerous voice

TAKE MY HAND

an outstretched hand
    such a simple gesture
    yet for us so monumental
    for i know that once
    i place my palm in yours
    and your gloved fingers
    close over mine
    i am captured
    and become your willing prisoner

blinding walking into
    the world of your creation
    fed with beautiful
    illusions that shimmer
    before my eyes

your smooth tenor
    calls my name

    alas, i cannot fight the pull
    i want to crawl inside the voice
    and live within it forever
    letting it stroke my hair
    contouring to its magnetic pull

—take my hand

DRAWN

blood thrumming
    underneath the
    starlight

the majestic moon
    witness to the frantic
    beating of my
    heart
    as you lean closer to me
    your breath tickling my neck
    hot and thick
    i feel the passion
    emanating from your skin
    it consumes me

how i fear you!
    and yet...

KAYLA LOWE

how drawn i am
to your presence

—drawn

YOUR SPIRIT AND MY VOICE

trilling up and down
    scaling keys i never
    knew i could achieve

your eyes gleam at me
    from beyond the mystery
    that is your masked visage
    with the approval that
    i so desperately need and long for

then they darken
    and you prowl
    stalking me with feminine grace

breathe in
    breathe out
    inhale

    exhale
    your hand
    pressing against my abdomen
    instructing me
    pulling me back against you

i gasp
    you prompt
    again!
    i open my mouth
    and my soul soars
    as our voices meld together
    in true love's song
    your spirit flowing through me

—your spirit and my voice

PLUCKING THE SOUL

like a master pianist you stroke
    the keys of my soul

your melody lingers with me even now
    haunting me

up on the arpeggio
    fevered, harried, full of anger, turmoil, madness
    and so many emotions
    my head pounds

then down on the adagio
    longing, tender, lamenting
    'til my heart pains me
    within my breast
    and pricks like a thousand
    tiny needles poked right through

    going beyond my heart
    to my hidden soul

filling me with fear and wonder simultaneously
    but perhaps what most disturbs me
    is how much I long to be in your presence again

—plucking the soul

NIGHT DUST

my heart longs for sleep
    for in my dreams
    i hear your
    angelic voice

it whispers to me
    words of love
    that give me images
    of myself
    floating on the wings
    of a pearl white dove

that chirps and sings
    a morning song
    blending into night dust
    that explodes and twinkles
    down as i fall back into my body

            . . .

KAYLA LOWE

—night dust

SHADOWS OF THE NIGHT

although i'm a child of daylight
    something in the smoky darkness
    speaks to me...

my heart thrills at the mystery
    and shivers of anticipation at the unknown
    race up and down my spine

i wish i could fly
    into the night
    like a great winged bat
    and discover all the mysteries
    that it holds from the children of the sun

  —shadows of the night

TAINTED LIGHT

you say that i am the light in your darkness
    yet there must be a companion darkness
    within me

for I am drawn inexplicably to you
    in a manner that both frightens and excites me
    i cannot fight it
    no matter how hard i try

i will return to you
    time and time again

you have stolen my soul—or no
    perhaps the black part of my soul
    answers the cry from your dark heart

        . . .

regardless you place me on too high a pedestal
    i am not purity
    i am a tainted light

just an orphan, a slip of a girl
    lost and wandering

—tainted light

FOREVER AND A DAY

wilt thou love me
    forever and a day?
    thou asketh me so sweetly

i reply that i will love thee always
    and peck thy cheek ever so neatly

the sun is brighter because of thy love
    flower more fragrant and berries sweeter
    mine soul took flight
    upon the wings of a dove

our love rivals the ones of lore
    music
    fills my mind when thou art near

        . . .

with thee, mine heart sings
    thy heart to me endear
    and joy thy adoration brings

wilt thou love me
    forever too
    as unchanging as the sea?
    If thou answereth yes
    my soul i present to thee!

—forever and a day

PRYING PANDORA

flickering flames
    reflected in
    a dark glassy lake
    the warm smell
    of wax dripping
    from candelabras
    that flank
    a magnificent pipe organ

the voice that lived
    in my dreams for so long
    finally took form
    in broad shoulders
    and a masked visage

but what lies
    beyond the mask?

. . .

—prying pandora

ERIK

LIGHT IN THE DARK

darkness abounds
    endless night
    his soul despairs
    until he loses hope
    and then...then...
    a light in the darkness
    its iridescent glow
    framing a face
    shrouded in curls, grace
    and innocence

—light in the dark

WE WILL SING

the day starts
    the sun rises
    time is ours
    hearts being faster
    than ever before
    each moment cherished
    our love will never perish
    we will sing
    and weeks pass
    and months pass
    seasons fly
    being with you makes my soul soar
    and in a daze
    we pass the joy-filled days
    we will sing forevermore
    and sometimes at night-time
    our music fills the air
    it swirls all around us in this once cold lair
    my broken soul is now alive and whole

please say you'll sing with me
forevermore

—we will sing

HER ESSENCE

her essence was a
    heady mix of
    roses and lavender
    her presence sweet
    and calming like
    the innocent melody
    of softly struck
    piano keys
    fingers twitching
    longing to touch her
    and feel her porcelain skin
    surely just that simple contact
    would elicit the grandest
    of sensations
    oh, just to touch
    her essence!

—her essence

CHARCOAL STAINS

pen and ink
    combining to create
    vibrant images
    imprinted on paper
    and canvas like
    the image of
    thine smile imprinted
    on mine tattered soul
    no vibrancy of colour
    could do justice
    to thy countenance though
    and no matter how many
    times i stroke thy
    drawn likeness
    my fingers come away
    with nothing but
    charcoal stains

    —charcoal stains

ILLUSION

i pray, my love
    that you will believe
    this illusion myself
    lovingly concocted for thee
    where thou art not thyself
    and i...god i, am not me
    in this otherworldly realm
    we can be what we want to be
    without the hurt
    without the pain
    where once upon a time
    our story will never end
    where i loveth thee
    and thee loveth me
    our hearts entwined
    and souls set free

—illusion

FIRE DANCE

let's dance into the fire
    we won't get burned
    when we become
    one with the flame
    we can burn
    with wild ferocity
    in our swirling madness
    and ravaging passions
    shining brighter
    than the sun
    blinding all who
    dare stare at us
    with our blazing light

—fire dance

LOVELIGHT

thy love is the light
    in my eternal darkness
    it sprinkles my night
    with beautiful starlight
    that puts twinkles
    in mine eyes
    and glowing embers
    in my black heart
    such light my
    broken soul
    has never known
    i stand awed
    by its luminescence

—lovelight

HEAVENLY LIGHT

thou art the sun
    that shines so bright
    breaking through the
    clouds of my darkness
    i want to reach out and touch
    thy beauty and yet I know that
    one with a soul as black and ugly
    as mine has no right to approach one
    as divine, good, pure, and heaven-sent as thee

—heavenly light

THE ANGEL IN HELL

a broken soul
    longing to be whole
    a wounded heart
    yearning to love
    an angel in the darkness
    shunned by the light
    beauty beyond compare
    artifice reigns in the lair
    the angel in hell
    despair not
    for redemption cometh
    in the form of angel's wings
    upon a heavenly voice
    a kindred spirit
    ensconced in curls and grace

—the angel in hell

POSSESSION

light and pure
    as if floating on a cloud
    your voice
    calling to my soul
    echoing my own spirit
    coaxing it forth
    and giving it wings
    to fly above the heavens
    only i will instruct
    when it joins with mine
    spiritual experience
    a sense of euphoria
    angels weep
    as do i
    for now i know
    i can never let you go
    you are mine
    all mine

                  . . .

KAYLA LOWE

—possession

DRUNK WITH LOVE

i am drunk
    and your voice is the wine
    like a glutton i want more and more
    i don't know when to stop
    don't fault me for my selfishness, my love
    for if you could only see yourself
    through my eyes you'd understand
    the meaning you give
    to my dreary existence

—drunk with love

FLOATING ON HIGH E

floating on high E
    musical notes
    others only dream
    of reaching
    pure coloratura
    trilling up and down
    the cadenza
    until it bursts
    in blinding sparkles
    setting my auditory
    senses aflame
    soliciting responses
    from my entire body
    i'm tinkling
    shaking from the power
    of the voice we created

—floating on high E

WHITE

white
    the only color
    i see for thee
    is white
    thy alabaster skin
    almost glowing
    in beautiful paleness
    creamy as fresh milk
    white lace and chiffon
    floating down thy figure
    pooling at thy feet
    in a delicate gauzy mass
    a single blood red rose
    only brings out
    the pink and red hues of
    thy lips and cheeks
    turning thee from
    a dream to
    a living bride
    shrouded in white

KAYLA LOWE

> white that pales
> in comparison
> and looks dirty
> next to thy purity

—white

OBSESSION

fear not, my love
    for the angel of music
    has thee under his wings
    he will watch over thee
    and guide thee
    his palm gently
    supporting thee as
    thou soarest higher and higher
    no harm cometh to thee, my love
    for fear of mine vengeance
    thy avenging angel he'll be
    if need be
    angel of music
    and angel of death
    all for thee

—obsession

COME WHAT MAY

thy countenance lit with joy
    ah, doth thou hear it?
    mine voice flitting from ear to ear
    it's here
    no it's here
    these little games
    bring thee such simple joy
    i would play them with thee always
    for the reward of thy gladness
    mine heart swells
    with love for thee
    until it's almost painful
    threatening to break forth
    from mine chest
    i cannot temper it
    nay, nor do i want to anymore
    let come what may

—come what may

IN THE BLEAK MIDWINTER

CHRISTINE

MASQUERADE

hooded eyes
    grins and lies
    skirts sway and billow
    faces spinning, covered in masks
    her footsteps stumble
    she's lost
    in a never-ending masquerade

—masquerade

HEAD OVER HEART

my heart is ever in contrast
    with my mind
    though my mind is wiser
    and screams the hard truth at me
    my heart whispers the deception
    lulling me into what i want to believe

i know what i should want
    and i know what i do want
    most of the time
    until that voice
    that voice
    calls to me
    distorting my reality

oh, that i could find an
    amicable balance

between these two most essential
halves of my being

—head over heart

TORN

you'd think it would be twice the fun
    but it's double the trouble
    loving two people
    instead of one

my heart is torn
    and my mind is confused

both keep telling me that i must choose
    am i going to stay
    with the one who loves me
    or go back
    to the one i love?

—torn

CHANGED

there are days i desperately long
    for those summers by the sea
    feeling the cool spray of the water
    misting my sun-kissed cheeks
    as i listen to the waves
    crashing upon the shore

it was just
    you and me
    and we were unbelievably happy
    but then a darkness appeared
    sucking us under and changing us into
    different people

we would never be the same again

—changed

YOUR LOVE

please don't make me love you
    your love is
    a dream
    and a nightmare

the beginning
    of heartbreak
    the end
    of innocence

it offers
    hope and despair
    pleasure and pain
    a bit of sunshine
    but a lot of rain

. . .

KAYLA LOWE

you'll steal my summers
    commandeer my mornings
    condemn me to the darkness
    until i wilt like a flower

—your love

TWISTED

knarled and tangled
    twisting every which way
    that is what
    our love
    has become

ours is not a smooth and beautiful
    aesthetically pleasing love

instead it's riddled
    with twists and turns
    that make it
    ugly
    and yet
    we are intricately entwined
    i can't break free
    no matter how hard i try

do i even want to?

—twisted

TOXIC LOVE

i fell in love with the devil
    unwittingly, of course
    our love for music bound us together

no difference in age or appearance
    could separate us
    for i was a slave to his voice
    jumping at his every whim
    and he showed me worlds i never imagined
    but in his desperation for light
    he sucked the soul out of me
    until all that was left was
    darkness
    and i was a shell of who i once was

his toxic love drained me until i felt
    as if i too were living in the darkest depths

KAYLA LOWE

    of hell

—toxic love

DEVOUR ME

you can travel
    to the ends of the earth

you can obtain
    the wealth of the world

you can take
    the power of the nations
    but will it ever be enough?

no...
    i think not

you will only be satisfied
    when you've

    devoured me
    destroying all that i am

—devour me

THE GREAT DIVIDE

here we stand
    on the precipice
    of the great divide

will we venture
    left or right
    towards
    darkness and unending night
    or
    sunlight and those summers by the sea?

—the great divide

THUNDERSTORM

the wind howls and mimics
    the cry of my soul

a familiar song plays
    and makes my heart bleed
    with fond remembrances
    of yesterdays
    and another time

i relish the thunder
    that commiserates with me
    and the rain that mirrors
    my own tears
    cleansing me

maybe by the time

the storm abates
my doubts will be
washed away
until i know my own heart

—thunderstorm

NIGHTMARES

memories of you have left me
    with nothing but
    nightmares

remembrances of your touch inspire
    fear

reliving the pain
    night after night

your voice which once
    excited my heart with
    gladness

now causes it to leap in
    terror

. . .

will anything ever be enough
    to make the nightmares go away?
    or will you always be there?
    singing songs in my head...

—nightmares

WOE

i've brought you nothing but
    woe
    yet you still want to
    float with me on this sea called life

either you truly do
    love me
    or you're as confused as i am

chained to a monster
    i can never be free

my heart and soul will never be whole
    you know this and yet you are still prepared
    to pitch your lot with mine
    woe is me

        . . .

—woe

CHAINS

my mind tells me
    i should love you

you truly do love me like no other
    you are everything i ever dreamed of

yet
    i am a fool
    and i cannot help it
    for i am in love with another

he's a monster
    some say pure evil

he stalks me in the corridors
    no matter where i go

    he's always there
    in my mind
    my head is filled with his sighs
    i sense his anger, his disapproval
    his pleasure
    oh, his pleasure!

he hurts me in every possible way
    but still i cannot quell the love within my heart
    even while i hate him simultaneously

could it be that ours is
    the truest kind of love?
    born out of the deepest of passions?

or am i ever deceived
    by the demon that is him?

oh, that i could break these chains!
    that bind me to his
    tortured soul!

—chains

GUILT

forgive me
    i beg you

don't make it end
    like this

unmasked, madness
    searing pain, your howl of rage
    maniacal laughter

my god
    have you gone mad?

i supplicate to the angel i once knew
    he's in there somewhere
    i know it

. . .

please hear my cry!
    don't tell me this crack in personality
    is permanent
    and my fault
    all my fault!

—guilt

CLIFF HANGER

fear
    enclosing on my throat
    i can't breathe
    suffocating

can i dive off the cliff
    into the pool that is your love?
    i don't think i could stand it

yet can i stand to be the cause
    of more pain
    of murder?

sacrifice grant me courage
    to take that plunge

          . . .

—cliff hanger

ERIK

ERIK

I PLUCKED A ROSE

i plucked a flower from the lane
    it was a rose of rarest bloom
    i plucked it in hopes of seeing thee again
    i took it to mine lonely tomb
    where it received the utmost care
    i held out hope that thou would come soon
    yet time did pass and i did despair
    the rose, it wilted and it died
    it couldn't take the cold dank air
    in my heart of hearts i knew thou lied
    when thou promised to return to mine side

—i plucked a rose

TAINTED SOUL

i've committed horrible acts
    acts that cause me
    to hang my head in shame
    at their recollection
    my soul is tainted;
    i'm a monster
    yet you see a sliver
    of good left in me
    just a tiny sliver and
    you love me all the same
    despite my darkness
    yet i know that darkness
    is engulfing
    i wonder how long
    until it consumes
    this light

—tainted soul

REGRETS

fingers of the past
    delve into my brain
    making me relive the horror
    of what i once was
    my actions fill me with shame
    the heartless cruelty
    and selfish devotion
    a slave to vice
    i sought comfort in all
    the wrong places
    and paid dearly for it
    the price of sin is high
    oh, that i had never paid it!

—regrets

NEVER BE FREE

curse you!
    damn you!
    and that insatiable curiosity
    like a cat
    you must have nine lives
    to still be breathing
    in my presence
    oh, my foolish child
    what have you done?
    what have you done?
    lock you away and
    throw away the key
    now you will never be free
    never be free

—never be free

BETRAYAL

ardently whispered promises
    stolen kisses atop the roof
    as if you think you're in heaven
    floating upon the clouds
    with all the mortals of Paris
    below you, worshipping you
    and i…
    i was a dog at your feet
    ready to give my life for you
    now in the shadows i skulk
    to the betrayal
    oh, the heart-wrenching pain!
    to witness it
    i want to rip my eyes from my skull
    this skull
    this death's head that's to blame
    for the treachery before me
    my chest constricts in the cold winter air
    i can't breathe as i struggle to contain

    the howl that builds within me
    like a wounded animal rent to the core

—betrayal

HATRED

that smug smile
    that i want to eradicate
    sneering as i watch you
    bow with what you think
    is gallantry
    a slave to fashion, a fop
    not worthy to lick the sole
    of her boot
    so assured in your privilege
    it's sickening to behold
    foolish boy
    you know not who
    you tangle with
    or what dangerous
    hatred you kindle

    —hatred

SPIRIT CRY

o my angel!
    how can you waste your talent
    that glorious voice that
    you and i honed together
    throw it all away
    on one as insolent
    and pallid as him?
    i will make you more
    than a prima donna
    under my tutelage
    you will become a goddess
    my little ingenue
    don't you know my spirit
    is contained within your voice?
    while it's your pure tone
    they love, it's the voice
    the cry of my spirit
    they truly hear

              . . .

—spirit cry

IN MY REALM

let me drape you
    in fine Persian silks
    don't cry my dear
    your chains are still mine
    or have you forgotten
    in your play time
    parading about the opera house
    with the boy
    oh, you thought i didn't know?
    i chuckle
    my child, here in my realm
    i see all
    don't let fear light your eyes
    just because you now know
    i know of your betrayal
    you were so happy and carefree
    in your believed deception
    which truly lets me know
    how little you think of me

once an angel
i am now no longer even
considered mortal worthy
enough of your refusal

—in my realm

THE POINT OF NO RETURN

rip my music
    to shreds
    these notes
    will never be played
    we'll bury them with us
    don juan triumphant
    i'll triumph in the end
    one way or the other
    i will have you
    if not as a living bride
    then in death be wed
    the choice is yours my darling
    a breathing wedding
    or one in the afterlife?
    this is the point of no return

—the point of no return

YOUR LOVE

rage, blinding rage
    a feral cry bursts forth
    from the pits of my black soul
    i hear it from afar
    and then realize it came
    from mine own throat
    fingernails tearing at skin
    blood trickling down this
    loathsome visage
    the source of my contempt
    the catalyst of my despair
    fear and loathing
    no, i don't want your pity silly girl!
    it's your love
    your love is all i want
    that which i was always denied
    is that too much to ask?

—your love

CONSUMING LOVE

ours is the kind of love that consumes
    you heart and soul
    it's fire and ice
    love and hate
    born from the deepest of passions
    and it'll drive you insane
    and send you to heaven and back in turns
    it's torture as much as it is bliss
    and you'll burn in its flames
    before i ever set you free

—consuming love

THE DEVIL'S CHILD

trapped
    caged in
    bars pressing
    against his skin
    cold, dank
    claustrophobia
    anxiety
    panic
    whip, crack, lash
    hissing in pain
    sing, sing, sing
    songs of ugly countenance
    gypsy caravan
    salvation and imprisonment
    simultaneously
    the devil's child

—the devil's child

THE CORPSE BRIDE

my lies make wet tracks down your cheeks
    my heart pains within me until i harden it
    betrayal, deceiving Delilah, no mercy
    catgut smooth yet rough in my fingers
    granting me power
    they want a show?
    let's give them one
    the grasshopper or the scorpion?
    i know what she'll choose
    it's probably for the best
    blow the fop up
    smithereens for us all then
    my lovely corpse bride
    her dress tattered and torn
    lovely even with her tear-stained cheeks
    we'll make our tomb here, my love

—the corpse bride

CLIMAX

oh sensation! sweet sensation!
    in my wildest fantasies
    i never imagined it would feel like this
    your little lips pressed against mine
    the sweetest burning nectar
    and my heart finally breaks
    completely in two
    that last fissure holding it in one piece
    torn away by your moment of sacrifice
    your act of kindness
    has crippled me
    so that i can't stand
    falling at your feet
    weeping into the hem
    of your dress
    on the Persian rug
    i know you love the boy
    and i cannot keep you
    no matter how much i want to
    i haven't the strength

KAYLA LOWE

    there are no words
    no thoughts
    go
    just go

—climax

LOST

she was
    his heart
    and soul
    and without her
    he couldn't breathe
    his will
    lost

—lost

RAOUL

IS SHE TEMPTED?

white
    the color of purity and grace

angels and halos
    cleanliness within

yet even white auras are sometimes
    drawn to dark ones black as sin

is the pull due to temptation?
    or for redemption's sake?

only time will tell whether
    the light will outshine the darkness
    or become swallowed

KAYLA LOWE

    in its vastness

—is she tempted?

VANISHED

where are you, my love?
    wilt thou answer the door?
    my concern growth

murmured voices
    a stirring within
    i press my ear to the door
    another man's voice!
    bursting forth into
    an empty space

but this cannot be!
    you were just here
    to whence have thou disappeared?

—vanished

PASSION PLAY

my heart is slowing breaking
    as i witness the scene playing about before me

my little lotte
    deny it as she might
    but she feels something for her angel, that demon
    more than what she professes

the way she goes to him
    as if in a trance
    without any verbal command
    being spoken between them
    the silent passion play is killing me

what is this power he has over her?

        . . .

—passion play

LITTLE LOTTE'S WANDERINGS

little lotte how your mind did always wander
    however in all its wanderings
    i never believed it'd take you so far
    as to be unwittingly taken in
    by such a man

a foul thing skulking in the shadows
    like a rat, hideous to behold

oh, my sweet innocent darling
    how could you ever have seen
    any good in a creature so repulsive?

sometimes you are too good
    for even your own good
    wanting to believe the best of everyone

and everything will lead to nothing
but trouble when you do so in vain

—little lotte's wanderings

THAT VOICE

naiveté, naiveté, your blasted naiveté!
    voices in the walls
    following wherever you are
    inside your head

i curse your father
    his fanciful tales and dark stories

angel of music indeed
    more like a predator
    a madman
    hiding within the vaults
    of the theatre
    hypnotizing you
    entrancing you
    enslaving you blinding
    to a voice

              . . .

a voice!
> devil take that voice!

—that voice

DUEL

frustration floods me
    the woman i love
    in danger with me
    helpless to protect her

how does one fight
    an unseen entity?

he's tipped all the
    scales in his favor
    in a cheating move
    the blackguard

come out and
    face me like a man

               . . .

i challenge you to a duel

—duel

I WILL BE YOUR LIGHT

she trembles in my arms
    shaking like a leaf
    the tiniest wind would be
    enough to blow her away

hollowed eyes and a thin frame

she's stopped eating in her distress
    he scares her

she begs me to protect her
    i vouch to do so with my life
    i'll whisk her away from here
    at the earliest opportunity
    i'll give her back her freedom
    and save her from the night

            . . .

i will be her light

she calms within my arms
    until a sigh carried on the gentle breeze
    set her nerves alight again
    causing her to cower like a frightened animal

—i will be your light

DOES SHE LOVE HIM?

she loves me
    i know she does
    when our lips meet

yet the tiniest whisper
    from one voice
    is enough to make her
    momentarily forget all
    promises made to me

she's a slave to it
    imprisoned by it

but is she a victim
    or a willing participant?

        . . .

i reprimand my mind
>   for entertaining the thought
>   but there are times
>   i fear that her fear
>   of the monster
>   is actually born
>   of a greater, deeper form
>   of affection that's actually
>   a testament to the deepest
>   kind of love

—does she love him?

RELEASE HER

you fiend! you rascal!
    leave her be!

you can't win her love
    by enslaving her with your voice

give her a choice
    for God's sake!
    release her from this torment

can't you see what it's doing to her?

—release her

IN THE VAULTS

mine eyes must deceive me
    cobwebs and darkness everywhere
    i squint to make out the faintest form

who would choose to live here?
    in the cold
    in the dank
    only something sub-human

cobwebs sticking to my hair
    the sound of dripping water
    beating in my heart
    filling my mind with wet fear

the cellars are maddening
    i too would surely go mad
    if i were to dwell here for long

KAYLA LOWE

. . .

my love
    my poor love
    trapped deep in these vaults
    with that creature from hell

—in the vaults

WITNESSING THE KISS

his twisted lips upon thine!
    i can't banish the image from mine eyes
    or quell the bile that threatens
    to rise within me just at the memory

more distinctly the gut-wrenching
    feeling in the pit of my stomach
    when thee chose

yes chose!

to kiss the monster a second time
    of thine own free will

clutching him to your bosom
    as he sobbed and clung to thee

    thy sweet crystal tears
    falling to mingle with his
    in an action so intimate

i felt as if i were the intruder
    on a private lover's scene-play

—witnessing the kiss

TORMENTED BY LOVE

you do love him!
    just admit it
    there's not point
    in your mouth denying
    what your eyes so clearly say

even if they say it
    regretfully, mournfully

you might not want to
    but a part of you
    does love him little lotte

a part of your heart
    that you've bestowed
    upon another and that
    i'll never have

KAYLA LOWE

. . .

you share a love
    of music with him

something that i cannot
    share with you

i cannot even begin
    to express the torment
    this causes me

tormented by
    the love i see in your eyes

—tormented by love

ENSNARED

once again she is his
    returned to his voice
    like a pet that answers
    the call of its master

she basks in his attention
    in his affection with his
    voice loving down upon her

wandering child
    returned to her angel
    he carries the music
    that is her heart

but he is a monster
    a demon!

i must save her from his snare!

—ensnared

DROWNING

gurgling
    sputtering
    can't breathe
    can't think
    the water
    rushing up to my nostrils

i'm drowning
    drowning for love
    i'd gladly drown
    if i knew it would free
    thee from his clutches

—drowning

LOVE TESTED

what happened to us?
    we were once so in love
    eager to never be parted

now we bicker and fight
    easily irritated by every nuance

you don't understand me anymore
    nor i you, or did we ever?

perhaps this is it,
    the beginning of the end…

but then our eyes meet
    and we see glimmers

of those people we fell in love with
and I know that ours is a love
that can weather the storms of life

—love tested

ABOUT THE AUTHOR

Award-winning author Kayla Lowe writes new adult fiction with a purpose. Her stories explore psychological and spiritual issues in relatable narratives that tug at the heartstrings and inspire self-reflection. Kayla is a Tennessee native who believes "writing is a way of life."

At age fifteen, she was among the youngest of Tennessee students to ever attend Tennessee's Governor's School for the Humanities, and at age sixteen, she began writing her first novel, the Christian romance, *Maiden's Blush*. An avid reader herself, she enjoys novels about the Phantom of the Opera as well as an eclectic mix of fiction and nonfiction. Kayla has been a freelance writer since 2007, and she was one of the "Top 100 Writers on Yahoo! Voices" in 2011. In 2017, she became a professional editor. She's an editor by day and writer by night who likes to occasionally dabble in poetry.

The first book in her Tainted Love saga, *Of Love and Deception*, received the Gold Award in New Adult Fiction in the 2021 Global Ebook Awards.

Kayla loves hearing from her readers. You can connect with her at her website: www.kaylalowe.com.